G000108616

Friendship

RUNNING PRESS
PHILADELPHIA · LONDON

Library of Congress Control Number: 2004110428

ISBN 0-7624-2347-1

This book may be ordered by mail from the publisher.
Please include $1.00 for postage and handling.
But try your bookstore first!

Running Press Book Publishers
125 South Twenty-second Street
Philadelphia, Pennsylvania 19103-4399

Log onto www.specialfavors.com to order Running Press®
Miniature Editions™ with your own custom-made covers!

Visit us on the web!
www.runningpress.com

Introduction

Who knows us better than our friends? Friends share with us, count on us, and comfort us. They improve the quality of our lives, raise our spiritual standard of living, and are not too polite to tell us when we have a bit of thread dangling from one sleeve.

When we're with them, we don't have to dress up, or put out the guest towels, or even finish our sentences. Friends know us better than that.

Through the quotations in this book, some of the world's greatest writers, thinkers, leaders, and celebrities—from Jane Austen to J.D. Salinger, and from Oprah

Winfrey to Mao Tse-tung—express their views on friendship. They embrace its sweetness, respect its scarcity, and occasionally pucker at its tang.

Each friendship is unique, but the need for friends and the pleasures of friendship are universal.

Friends do not live in harmony merely, as some say, but in melody.

—HENRY DAVID THOREAU (1817–1862)
AMERICAN WRITER

SOME OF MY BEST FRIENDS ARE
CHILDREN. IN FACT, ALL OF MY
BEST FRIENDS ARE CHILDREN.

—J.D. SALINGER (B. 1919)
AMERICAN WRITER

Love is friendship set on fire.

—JEREMY TAYLOR (1613–1667)
ENGLISH BISHOP AND THEOLOGICAL WRITER

GRIEF CAN TAKE CARE OF ITSELF,
BUT TO GET THE FULL VALUE OF
A JOY YOU MUST HAVE SOMEBODY
TO DIVIDE IT WITH.

—MARK TWAIN (1835–1910)
AMERICAN WRITER

There are three types of friends: those like food, without which you can't live; those like medicine, which you need occasionally; and those like an illness, which you never want.

—SOLOMON IBN GABIROL (1021–1058)
HEBREW POET AND APHORIST

If you have one true friend you have more than your share.

—THOMAS FULLER (1654–1734)
ENGLISH PHYSICIAN AND WRITER

A FRIEND IS ONE WHO
DISLIKES THE SAME PEOPLE
YOU DISLIKE.

—ANONYMOUS

It is said that love is blind. Friendship, on the other hand, is clairvoyant.

—PHILIPPE SOUPAULT (1897–1990)
FRENCH WRITER

PLATONIC LOVE IS LOVE FROM THE NECK UP.

friends
forever!

—THYRA SAMTER WINSLOW (1903–1961)
AMERICAN DRAMA AND LITERARY CRITIC

*I get by with
a little help from
my friends.*

—John Lennon (1940–1980)
English musician and writer

*Think where man's glory
most begins and ends,
And say my glory was
I had such friends.*

—WILLIAM BUTLER YEATS (1865–1939)
IRISH POET AND DRAMATIST

Having someone wonder where you are when you don't come home at night is a very old human need.

—MARGARET MEAD (1901–1978)
AMERICAN ANTHROPOLOGIST

DIAMONDS ARE A GIRL'S
BEST FRIEND.

—LEO ROBIN (1900–1984)
AMERICAN SONGWRITER

AFTER AN ACQUAINTANCE
OF TEN MINUTES MANY
WOMEN WILL EXCHANGE
CONFIDENCES THAT A
MAN WOULD NOT REVEAL
TO A LIFELONG FRIEND.

—PAGE SMITH (B. 1917)
AMERICAN HISTORIAN

We tiptoed around each other like heartbreaking new friends.

—JACK KEROUAC (1922–1969)
AMERICAN WRITER

I DO NOT WANT PEOPLE TO
BE VERY AGREEABLE, AS IT
SAVES ME THE TROUBLE OF
LIKING THEM A GREAT DEAL.

—JANE AUSTEN (1775–1817)
ENGLISH WRITER

MY FRIENDS,
THERE ARE NO FRIENDS.

—COCO CHANEL (1883–1971)
FRENCH FASHION DESIGNER

Friendship is far more tragic than love. It lasts longer.

—OSCAR WILDE (1854–1900)
IRISH POET AND DRAMATIST

Most people enjoy the inferiority of their friends.

—LORD CHESTERFIELD (1694–1773)
ENGLISH STATESMAN AND WRITER

EACH HAD HIS PAST SHUT IN
HIM LIKE THE LEAVES OF A BOOK
KNOWN TO HIM BY HEART;
AND HIS FRIENDS COULD ONLY
READ THE TITLE.

—VIRGINIA WOOLF (1882–1941)
ENGLISH WRITER

If I had to choose between betraying my country and betraying my friend, I hope I should have the guts to betray my country.

—E.M. FORSTER (1879–1970)
ENGLISH WRITER

When people have light in themselves, it will shine out from them. Then we get to know each other as we walk together in the darkness, without needing to pass our hands over each other's faces, or to intrude into each other's hearts.

—ALBERT SCHWEITZER (1875–1965)
GERMAN SCHOLAR AND HUMANITARIAN

THESE CAN NEVER BE TRUE
FRIENDS: HOPE, DICE,
A PROSTITUTE, A ROBBER,
A CHEAT, A GOLDSMITH,
A MONKEY, A DOCTOR,
A DISTILLER.

—HINDU PROVERB

*Choose
an author
as you choose
a friend.*

—WENTWORTH DILLON, EARL OF
ROSCOMMON (1633–1685)
ENGLISH NOBLEMAN

We all take different paths in life, but no matter where we go, we take a little of each other everywhere.

—TIM MCGRAW (B. 1967)
AMERICAN COUNTRY SINGER

*Treat people as if they
were what they ought to be,
and you help them to
become what they are
capable of being.*

—JOHANN WOLFGANG VON GOETHE
(1749–1832)
GERMAN DRAMATIST AND POET

PERHAPS ONLY PEOPLE WHO
ARE CAPABLE OF REAL
TOGETHERNESS HAVE THAT
LOOK OF BEING ALONE IN
THE UNIVERSE ... THE
OTHERS HAVE A CERTAIN
STICKINESS.

—D.H. LAWRENCE (1885–1930)
ENGLISH WRITER

FRIENDSHIP IS ALMOST ALWAYS
THE UNION OF A PART OF ONE
MIND WITH A PART OF ANOTHER;
PEOPLE ARE FRIENDS IN SPOTS.

—GEORGE SANTAYANA (1863–1952)
AMERICAN WRITER

Treat your friends as you do your pictures, and place them in their best light.

—JENNIE JEROME CHURCHILL (1854–1921)
AMERICAN WRITER (MOTHER OF WINSTON
CHURCHILL)

Animals are such agreeable friends—they ask no questions, they pass no criticisms.

—GEORGE ELIOT (1819–1880)
ENGLISH WRITER

LOTS OF PEOPLE WANT TO
RIDE WITH YOU IN THE LIMO,
BUT WHAT YOU WANT IS SOME-
ONE WHO WILL TAKE THE BUS
WITH YOU WHEN THE LIMO
BREAKS DOWN.

—OPRAH WINFREY (B. 1954)
AMERICAN TV PERSONALITY AND ACTRESS

One passes through the world knowing few, if any, of the important things about even the people with whom one has been . . . in the closest intimacy.

—ANTHONY POWELL (1905–2000)
ENGLISH WRITER

One friend in a
lifetime is much;
two are many;
three are hardly
possible.

—HENRY ADAMS (1838–1918)
AMERICAN WRITER

*To find a friend,
one must close
one eye: to keep
him, two.*

—NORMAN DOUGLAS (1868–1952)
ENGLISH NOVELIST AND SCIENTIST

I'M NOT AFTER FAME AND
SUCCESS AND FORTUNE AND
POWER. IT'S MOSTLY [THAT I
WANT] TO HAVE A GOOD JOB
AND HAVE GOOD FRIENDS;
THAT'S THE GOOD STUFF IN LIFE.

—DREW BARRYMORE (B. 1975)
AMERICAN ACTRESS

Every murderer is probably somebody's old friend.

—AGATHA CHRISTIE (1890–1976)
ENGLISH WRITER

*Think twice
before you speak
to a friend
in need.*

*Friendship
is like money,
easier made
than kept.*

—SAMUEL BUTLER (1835–1902)
ENGLISH NOVELIST AND ESSAYIST

UNFORTUNATELY, IN A LONG
LIFE ONE GETS BARNACLED OVER
WITH THE MERE SHELLS OF
FRIENDSHIP AND IT IS DIFFICULT
WITHOUT HURTING ONESELF
TO SCRAPE THEM OFF.

—BERNARD BERENSON (1865–1959)
POLISH-AMERICAN ART CRITIC

INSTEAD OF LOVING YOUR
ENEMIES, TREAT YOUR FRIENDS
A LITTLE BETTER.

—EDGAR WATSON HOWE (1853–1937)
AMERICAN WRITER

The most I can do for my friend is simply be his friend.

—HENRY DAVID THOREAU (1817–1862)
AMERICAN WRITER

CONSTANT USE HAD NOT
WORN RAGGED THE FABRIC
OF THEIR FRIENDSHIP.

—DOROTHY PARKER (1893–1967)
AMERICAN WRITER AND LITERARY CRITIC

Love and friendship
are profoundly personal,
selfish values . . . an
expression and assertion
of self-esteem, a response
to one's own values in the
person of another.

—AYN RAND (1905–1982)
RUSSIAN-BORN AMERICAN WRITER

What I cannot love, I overlook. Is that real friendship?

—Anaïs Nin (1903–1977)
French-born American writer

HISTORIES ARE MORE FULL
OF EXAMPLES OF THE FIDELITY
OF DOGS THAN FRIENDS.

—ALEXANDER POPE (1688–1744)
ENGLISH POET

Only choose in marriage a woman whom you would choose as a friend if she were a man.

—JOSEPH JOUBERT (1754–1824)
FRENCH PHILOSOPHER

FRIENDSHIP ... IS NOT
SOMETHING YOU LEARN IN
SCHOOL. BUT IF YOU HAVEN'T
LEARNED THE MEANING OF
FRIENDSHIP, YOU REALLY
HAVEN'T LEARNED ANYTHING.

—MUHAMMAD ALI (B. 1942)
AMERICAN BOXER

To want friendship is a great fault. Friendship ought to be a gratuitous joy, like the joys afforded by art, or life . . .

—Simone Weil (1909–1943)
French philosopher

Money can't buy friends, but you can get a better class of enemy.

—SPIKE MILLIGAN (1918–2002)
ENGLISH COMEDIAN AND WRITER

I no more like people personally than I like dogs. When I meet them I am only apprehensive whether they will bite me, which is reasonable and sensible.

—STANLEY SPENCER (1891–1959)
ENGLISH ARTIST

We need two kinds of acquaintances, one to complain to, while we boast to the others.

—LOGAN PEARSALL SMITH (1865–1946)
ANGLO-AMERICAN WRITER

Fear makes strangers of people who would be friends.

—SHIRLEY MACLAINE (B. 1934)
AMERICAN ACTRESS

It is in the thirties that we want friends. In the forties we know they won't save us any more than love did.

—F. Scott Fitzgerald (1896–1940)
American writer

BECAUSE I GOT YOU TO
LOOK AFTER ME, AND YOU GOT
ME TO LOOK AFTER YOU . . . WE
GOT EACH OTHER, THAT'S WHAT,
THAT GIVES A HOOT IN HELL
ABOUT US . . .

—JOHN STEINBECK (1902–1968)
AMERICAN WRITER

A friend knows how to allow for mere quantity in your talk, and only replies to the quality . . .

—WILLIAM DEAN HOWELLS (1837–1920)
AMERICAN WRITER

IF YOU WANT A PERSON'S FAULTS, GO TO THOSE WHO LOVE HIM. THEY WILL NOT TELL YOU, BUT THEY KNOW.

—ROBERT LOUIS STEVENSON (1850–1894)
SCOTTISH WRITER

I CAN TRUST MY FRIENDS.
THESE PEOPLE FORCE ME
TO EXAMINE, ENCOURAGE
ME TO GROW.

—CHER (B. 1946)
AMERICAN SINGER AND ACTRESS

*And the song,
from beginning
to end, I found
in the heart of
a friend.*

—Henry Wadsworth Longfellow
(1807–1882)
American poet

There was nothing remote or mysterious here—only something private. The only secret was the ancient communication between two people.

—EUDORA WELTY (1909–2001)
AMERICAN WRITER

THERE CAN BE NO FRIENDSHIP
WHEN THERE IS NO FREEDOM;
FRIENDSHIP LOVES THE FREE
AIR, AND WILL NOT BE FENCED
UP IN STRAIGHT AND NARROW
ENCLOSURES.

—WILLIAM PENN (1644–1718)
ENGLISH QUAKER AND AMERICAN COLONY
FOUNDER

THERE'S A KIND OF EMOTIONAL
EXPLORATION YOU PLUMB WITH
A FRIEND THAT YOU DON'T
REALLY DO WITH YOUR FAMILY.

—BETTE MIDLER (B. 1945)
AMERICAN SINGER AND ACTRESS

THEY GREW TO BE SO HAPPY
THAT EVEN WHEN THEY WERE
TWO WORN-OUT OLD PEOPLE
THEY KEPT ON . . . PLAYING
TOGETHER LIKE DOGS.

—GABRIEL GARCÍA MÁRQUEZ (B. 1928)
COLOMBIAN WRITER

A COMPANION LOVES SOME
AGREEABLE QUALITIES WHICH A
MAN MAY POSSESS, BUT A FRIEND
LOVES THE MAN HIMSELF.

—JAMES BOSWELL (1740–1795)
SCOTTISH BIOGRAPHER AND LAWYER

The differences between friends cannot but reinforce their friendship.

—MAO TSE-TUNG (1893–1976)
CHINESE LEADER

The best way to mend a broken heart is time and girlfriends.

—GWYNETH PALTROW (B. 1972)
AMERICAN ACTRESS

A WOMAN WANTS HER
FRIENDS TO BE PERFECT. SHE
SETS A PATTERN . . . LAYS A
FRIEND OUT ON THIS PATTERN
AND WORRIES AND PRODS AT
ANY LITTLE QUALITIES WHICH
DO NOT COINCIDE WITH HER
OWN IMAGE.

—BETTY MacDONALD (1908–1958)
AMERICAN WRITER

The richer your friends, the more they will cost you.

—Elisabeth Marbury (1856?–1933)
American theatrical agent

Friendship is unnecessary, like philosophy, like art . . . It has no survival value; rather it is one of those things that give value to survival.

—C.S. LEWIS (1898–1963)
ENGLISH WRITER

I NO DOUBT DESERVED MY
ENEMIES, BUT I DON'T BELIEVE
I DESERVED MY FRIENDS.

—WALT WHITMAN (1819–1892)
AMERICAN POET

I HAVE LOST FRIENDS,
SOME BY DEATH, OTHERS
THROUGH SHEER INABILITY
TO CROSS THE STREET.

—VIRGINIA WOOLF (1882–1941)
ENGLISH WRITER

Friends are a second existence.

—Baltasar Gracian (1601–1958)
Spanish satirist and writer

A TRUE FRIEND IS SOMEONE
WHO LETS YOU HAVE TOTAL
FREEDOM TO BE YOURSELF—
AND ESPECIALLY TO FEEL.

—JIM MORRISON (1943–1974)
AMERICAN MUSICIAN AND POET

The only thing to do is hug one's friends tight and do one's job.

—EDITH WHARTON (1862–1937)
AMERICAN WRITER

IF TWO PEOPLE WHO LOVE EACH
OTHER LET A SINGLE INSTANT
WEDGE ITSELF BETWEEN THEM,
IT GROWS—IT BECOMES A
MONTH, A YEAR, A CENTURY;
IT BECOMES TOO LATE.

—JEAN GIRAUDOUS (1882–1944)
FRENCH PLAYWRIGHT

BEING WITH YOU IS LIKE
WALKING ON A VERY CLEAR
MORNING—DEFINITELY
THE SENSATION OF
BELONGING THERE.

—E.B. WHITE (1899–1985)
AMERICAN WRITER

It is good to have some friends both in Heaven and in Hell.

—GEORGE HERBERT (1593–1633)
ENGLISH WRITER

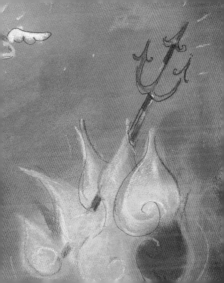

Friendship is a very taxing and arduous form of leisure activity.

—MORTIMER ADLER (1902–2001)
AMERICAN EDUCATOR

EACH FRIEND REPRESENTS A
WORLD IN US, A WORLD POSSIBLY
NOT BORN UNTIL THEY ARRIVE,
AND IT IS ONLY BY THIS MEETING
THAT A NEW WORLD IS BORN.

—ANAÏS NIN (1903–1977)
FRENCH-BORN AMERICAN WRITER

YOU HAVE TO LAUGH AND
CRY OVER AND OVER AGAIN
WITH SOMEONE BEFORE YOU
FEEL COMFORTABLE.

—JOAN RIVERS (B. 1933)
AMERICAN COMIC AND WRITER

I have learned that to be with those I like is enough.

—WALT WHITMAN (1819–1892)
AMERICAN WRITER

WHAT IS IMPORTANT TO A
RELATIONSHIP IS A HARMONY OF
EMOTIONAL ROLES AND NOT TOO
GREAT A DISPARITY IN THE GEN-
ERAL LEVEL OF INTELLIGENCE.

—MIRRA KOMAROVSKY (1905–1999)
RUSSIAN-AMERICAN EDUCATOR

The friends who grew up with you deserve a special respect. The ones who stuck by you shoulder to shoulder, in a time where nothing was certain, all life lay ahead, and every road led home.

—The Wonder Years
American TV sitcom

Friendship or love—one must choose. One cannot serve two masters.

—RENÉ CREVEL (1900–1935)
FRENCH WRITER

WHEREVER YOU ARE IT
IS YOUR OWN FRIENDS WHO
MAKE YOUR WORLD.

—WILLIAM JAMES (1842–1910)
AMERICAN PSYCHOLOGIST
AND PHILOSOPHER

WHEN A PERSON THAT ONE
LOVES IS IN THE WORLD AND
ALIVE AND WELL . . . THEN
TO MISS THEM IS ONLY A NEW
FLAVOR, A SALT SHARPNESS
IN EXPERIENCE.

—WINIFRED HOLTBY (1898–1935)
ENGLISH WRITER

The bird a nest,
the spider a web,
man friendship.

GO THROUGH YOUR PHONE BOOK, CALL PEOPLE AND ASK THEM TO DRIVE YOU TO THE AIRPORT. THE ONES WHO WILL DRIVE YOU ARE YOUR TRUE FRIENDS. THE REST AREN'T BAD PEOPLE; THEY'RE JUST ACQUAINTANCES.

—JAY LENO (B. 1950)
AMERICAN COMEDIAN AND TALK SHOW HOST

*The best way
to destroy an
enemy is to make
him a friend.*

—ABRAHAM LINCOLN (1809–1865)
AMERICAN PRESIDENT

A FRIEND IS ONE THAT KNOWS
YOU AS YOU ARE, UNDERSTANDS
WHERE YOU HAVE BEEN,
ACCEPTS WHAT YOU HAVE
BECOME, AND STILL, GENTLY
ALLOWS YOU TO GROW.

—WILLIAM SHAKESPEARE (1564–1616)
ENGLISH DRAMATIST AND POET

TRUE FRIENDSHIP IS AN IDENTITY OF SOULS RARELY TO BE FOUND IN THE WORLD. ONLY BETWEEN LIKE NATURES CAN FRIENDSHIPS BE ALTOGETHER WORTHY AND ENDURING.

—MOHANDAS GANDHI (1869–1948)
INDIAN SPIRITUAL LEADER

*The only way
to have a friend
is to be one.*

—RALPH WALDO EMERSON (1803–1882)
AMERICAN POET AND ESSAYIST

THAT IS WHAT FRIENDSHIP
MEANS. SHARING THE
PREJUDICE OF EXPERIENCE.

—CHARLES BUKOWSKI (1920–1994)
AMERICAN POET AND FICTION WRITER

*Friendship is
a sheltering tree.*

—SAMUEL TAYLOR COLERIDGE (1772–1834)
ENGLISH POET

TRUE FRIENDSHIP IS LIKE
SOUND HEALTH, THE VALUE
OF IT IS SELDOM KNOWN
UNTIL IT BE LOST.

—CHARLES CALEB COLTON (1780–1832)
ENGLISH WRITER AND CLERGYMAN

A MAN'S FRIENDSHIPS ARE
ONE OF THE BEST MEASURES
OF HIS WORTH.

—CHARLES DARWIN (1809–1882)
BRITISH NATURALIST

*There are some things
you can't share without
ending up like each
other, and knocking out
a twelve-foot mountain
troll is one of them.*

—J.K. ROWLING (B. 1965)
ENGLISH WRITER

It's not a lack of love, but a lack of friendship that makes unhappy marriages.

—FRIEDRICH NIETZSCHE (1844–1900)
GERMAN PHILOSOPHER

FRIENDS ARE GENERALLY
OF THE SAME SEX, FOR
WHEN MEN AND WOMEN
AGREE, IT IS ONLY IN THE
CONCLUSIONS; THEIR REASONS
ARE ALWAYS DIFFERENT.

—GEORGE SANTAYANA (1863–1952)
AMERICAN PHILOSOPHER AND POET

*The worst solitude
is to have no real
friendships.*

—FRANCIS BACON (1561–1626)
ENGLISH PHILOSOPHER, ESSAYIST,
AND STATESMAN

KEEP AWAY FROM PEOPLE
WHO TRY TO BELITTLE YOUR
AMBITIONS. SMALL PEOPLE
ALWAYS DO THAT, BUT THE
REALLY GREAT MAKE YOU
FEEL THAT YOU, TOO, CAN
BECOME GREAT.

—MARK TWAIN (1835–1910)
AMERICAN AUTHOR

YES'M, OLD FRIENDS IS ALWAYS
BEST, 'LESS YOU CAN CATCH
A NEW ONE THAT'S FIT TO
MAKE AN OLD ONE OUT OF.

—SARAH ORNE JEWETT (1849–1909)
AMERICAN WRITER

Friendship often ends in love; but love in friendship—never.

—Charles Caleb Colton (1780–1832)
English writer and clergyman

Louis, I think this is the beginning of a beautiful friendship.

RICK BLAINE
SALOON OWNER (IN THE FILM *CASABLANCA*)

THIS BOOK HAS BEEN BOUND USING
HANDCRAFT METHODS AND SMYTH-SEWN
TO ENSURE DURABILITY.

THE DUST JACKET AND INTERIOR
WERE ILLUSTRATED BY MARANDA MABERRY.

THE DUST JACKET AND INTERIOR WERE
DESIGNED BY GWEN GALEONE.

THE TEXT WAS EDITED BY
JENNIFER LECZKOWSKI.

THE TEXT WAS SET IN MINION, AND
BRUSH SCRIPT.